DON'T DO IT! DON'T DO IT! DON'T DO IT!

DON'T Do It! DON'T Do It! DON'T Do It!

Suicide Prevention Poems

Walter the Educator

SKB

Silent King Books a WhichHead Imprint

Copyright © 2023 by Walter the Educator

All rights reserved. No part of this book may be reproduced in any manner whatsoever without written permission except in the case of brief quotations embodied in critical articles and reviews.

First Printing, 2023

This book is a literary work; poems are not about specific persons, locations, situations, and/or circumstances unless mentioned in a historical context. This book is for entertainment and informational purposes only. Poems listed inside of this book do NOT provide a guarantee to prevent suicide. The author and publisher offer this information without warranties expressed or implied. No matter the grounds, neither the author nor the publisher will be accountable for any losses, injuries, or other damages caused by the reader's use of this book. The use of this book acknowledges an understanding and acceptance of this disclaimer.

for the people struggling

988 Suicide and Crisis Lifeline

By calling or texting 988, you'll connect with mental health professionals with the 988 Suicide and Crisis Lifeline.

CONTENTS

Dedication v

Why I Created This Book? 1

One - Dear Soul 2

Two - Conquer Every Fear 4

Three - Waiting To Be Free 6

Four - Don't Say Goodbye 8

Five - Battle Against Darkness 10

Six - Your Heart Will Restore 12

Seven - Worth Fighting For 14

Eight - Side By Side 16

Nine - Don't Lose Sight 18

Ten - Strength To Achieve 20

Eleven - Gentlest Of Sounds 22

Twelve - Reach Out 24

Thirteen - Strength Anew 26

Fourteen - You're Not Alone 28

Fifteen - Trust In Tomorrow 30

Sixteen - So Much More 32

Seventeen - Together We Are Strong . . . 34

Eighteen - Beacon Of Hope 36

Nineteen - We'll Rise And Learn To Cope . . 38

Twenty - Let Your Story Unfold 40

Twenty-One - Hold On 42

Twenty-Two - Cherished Pearl 44

Twenty-Three - Reason To Persevere . . . 46

Twenty-Four - Battle Is Won 48

Twenty-Five - Mending Your Heart 50

Twenty-Six - You Deserve To Stay 52

Twenty-Seven - Letting Healing Begin 54

Twenty-Eight - More Than Words 56

Twenty-Nine - Immeasurable 58

Thirty - Overcome The Pain 60

Thirty-One - Brand-new Day 62

Thirty-Two - Brighter Tomorrow 64

Thirty-Three - Unique Masterpiece 66

Thirty-Four - Resilience Resides 68

Thirty-Five - Tapestry Of Life 70

About The Author 72

WHY I CREATED THIS BOOK?

Creating a poetry book that encourages a person not to commit suicide serves as a powerful tool to provide hope, solace, and support to individuals who may be struggling with thoughts of self-harm. Poetry has the ability to convey complex emotions, offer understanding, and ignite a sense of connection with others. By exploring themes of resilience, self-love, and the beauty of life, this book can remind readers of their worth, inspire them to seek help, and provide a glimmer of hope in their darkest moments. It aims to promote empathy, raise awareness about mental health, and foster a compassionate dialogue around suicide prevention.

ONE

DEAR SOUL

In the depths of despair, when darkness looms,
And the weight of the world brings you to your knees,
Know that you're not alone in this endless gloom,
There's support and love, if only you seize.

Seek the lifeline that's there, just a call away,
Dial 988, let your voice be heard,
Confidential support, they'll guide you each day,
Through the tempestuous seas, they'll be your word.

When social media echoes with cries for help,
Reach out to the safety teams, their care is true,
They'll lend an ear, offer solace, and dispel,
The torment that haunts, they'll help you see through.

Suicide is a battle, a public health fight,
But statistics won't define your destiny,

Know the signs, the risks, and seek the light,
With healthcare providers, find serenity.

SAMHSA's locator, a beacon of hope,
Online resources to aid your way,
NIMH's research, knowledge to cope,
Together we'll forge a brighter day.

Hold on, dear soul, let hope be your guide,
There's strength in connection, love by your side,
Embrace the support, for life is worth living,
You're not alone, we're here, always giving.

TWO

CONQUER EVERY FEAR

In the depths of despair, when darkness looms,
And life's burdens weigh heavy, casting gloom,
Know that you're not alone, my friend,
For your pain, there's a helping hand to lend.

In this battle against the void within,
There's hope and strength waiting to begin.
Reach out, seek the light that shines so bright,
Hold on tight, for life's worth the fight.

The world may seem cold, devoid of care,
But look around, love is everywhere.
In every smile, every kind word spoken,
A reminder that you're not broken.

Embrace the warmth of a stranger's touch,
Let their compassion heal you, oh so much.

For in connection, lies the key,
To unlock the door, set your spirit free.

When the weight of the world becomes too great,
Remember, it's never too late,
To dial a helpline, seek a listening ear,
To find solace in the presence of those who care.

Online, there's a wealth of resources to explore,
Communities of support, ready to restore,
Your faith in the beauty of life's design,
With understanding hearts, they'll help you shine.

So, my dear friend, don't give up the fight,
Let hope guide you through the darkest night.
You are valued, loved, and needed here,
Together, we'll conquer every fear.

THREE

WAITING TO BE FREE

In the darkest depths where shadows dwell,
A weary soul cries out, lost in its own hell.
But listen, dear heart, for there is a way,
To find solace and hope, to see a brighter day.

Reach out your hand, let someone in,
For in the embrace of love, healing begins.
Speak your truth, let your pain be heard,
For there are those who'll listen, with every word.

In the depths of despair, you are not alone,
There are lifelines waiting, to guide you home.
Helplines, online resources, and caring hearts,
Ready to support, to mend the broken parts.

Hold on, my dear, to the strength within,
For you have the power to heal and begin.

Seek the light that still flickers in your soul,
Embrace the love, let it make you whole.
    You are important, you matter, you see,
There's a world of beauty, waiting to be free.
Hold onto hope, let it be your guide,
For in the darkest moments, love will provide.
    So, my dear, please stay, don't fade away,
Embrace the love that surrounds you each day.
Together we'll walk, hand in hand,
For you are cherished, you are loved, you're grand.

FOUR

DON'T SAY GOODBYE

In the darkest hours, when shadows loom,
And hope feels distant, lost in gloom,
Remember, dear soul, there's strength in you,
A light that shines, a love so true.

Though pain may grip your weary heart,
Hold on, my friend, don't fall apart,
For in this world, so vast and wide,
There are hands to hold you by your side.

Reach out, my dear, don't be afraid,
A lifeline's waiting, don't hesitate,
Helplines there, with open ears,
Ready to listen, to calm your fears.

The internet's embrace, a world of care,
Supportive voices, always there,

For in this digital realm we find,
Kindred spirits, hearts entwined.

Hold onto hope, let it guide your way,
For brighter skies will come, I say,
In every storm, a calm will rise,
And tears will dry, revealing blue skies.

You are important, cherished, loved,
A precious soul, sent from above,
Embrace the warmth that others bring,
And hear the song your heart can sing.

So please, my friend, don't say goodbye,
Let love and light help you defy,
The darkness that surrounds your mind,
And know, dear one, you're worth the find.

Hold tight, my dear, you'll see it through,
With love and hope, you'll start anew,
For in this journey we call life,
You'll find the strength to heal, to thrive.

FIVE

BATTLE AGAINST DARKNESS

In the depths of despair, when darkness surrounds,
A plea for hope, a gentle sound.
When burdens weigh heavy, and tears start to flow,
Please listen closely, there's something you should know.

You are not alone, though it may seem that way,
There's a world of care, waiting to light your way.
Reach out for help, let your voice be heard,
There are helplines, online resources, and the support of others.

Embrace the love that surrounds you, so pure,
The power of connection, a lifeline to endure.
Hold onto hope, let it guide your way,
For brighter tomorrows, just a step away.

You're stronger than you know, with courage deep within,
The battles you face, you have the strength to win.
Your worth is immeasurable, your light shines bright,
In a world that needs you, day and night.

Don't give in, don't let go,
There's so much more to see, so much more to know.
You have dreams to chase, and stories to tell,
In this journey called life, you have a place to dwell.

So stay, my friend, and face the storms with might,
For in your heart, the power to ignite.
Hold on to love, hold on to life's embrace,
There's healing and joy, in every single space.

Remember, you are cherished, you are adored,
You matter deeply, to this world and more.
Together we stand, hand in hand,
In the battle against darkness, we make our stand.

SIX

YOUR HEART WILL RESTORE

In the darkest hour, when shadows loom,
And despair engulfs you, consuming your room,
Hold on, my friend, for hope is near,
A lifeline awaits, a heart to hear.

In this vast universe, you're not alone,
A symphony of souls, all on their own,
But together we stand, united we'll be,
For love and support can set us free.

Your worth is immeasurable, beyond compare,
A shining light, a soul so rare,
Embrace the strength within your core,
And know that brighter days lie in store.

Seek out the hands that long to hold,
The ears that listen, the hearts so bold,

For in their warmth, you'll find solace and peace,
A haven of love, where your pain can cease.
    Remember, dear soul, you're here for a reason,
To touch lives, to paint the world with your season,
With every breath, you hold the power,
To make a difference, to bloom and flower.
    So let the tears fall, let the burdens release,
For we'll walk by your side, offering our peace,
Together we'll rise, beyond the despair,
For life's beauty awaits, if you're willing to dare.
    Hold on, my friend, let your spirit soar,
For in this journey, your heart will restore,
Reach out, embrace the love that surrounds,
For in that love, true healing abounds.

SEVEN

WORTH FIGHTING FOR

In the depths of despair, when shadows loom,
And darkness engulfs your heart in gloom,
Hold on, my dear, for hope is near,
A guiding light to banish your fear.

You are loved more than words can convey,
A cherished soul, with a purpose to sway,
Your presence, a gift, a beacon of light,
In this vast world, shining ever so bright.

Reach out your hand, let others embrace,
Their love and support, a saving grace,
For in connection, solace is found,
A lifeline to lift you from the ground.

Tears may fall, let them cleanse your soul,
Release the pain that takes its toll,

Seek help, dear one, it's a strength, not weak,
Resilience blooms when support you seek.

    Dreams await, stories yet to unfold,
A future of wonders, yet untold,
Your life is a canvas, a masterpiece,
Painted with love, hope will never cease.

    Hold on, stay strong, let love guide your way,
Through the darkest nights, to brighter days,
For you are important, cherished, and adored,
In this journey of life, you're worth fighting for.

    Remember, dear heart, you're never alone,
Together we'll heal, and hope will be sown,
Embrace the beauty that awaits, you see,
In life's embrace, love will set you free.

EIGHT

SIDE BY SIDE

In the darkest of nights, when shadows loom,
When the weight of the world feels like impending doom,
Hold on, my friend, don't let go of the thread,
For there's love in this world, waiting to be spread.
    Seek out a lifeline, a voice on the line,
A helpline, online resource, a friend so kind,
In their words, you'll find solace and care,
A reminder that you're cherished, beyond compare.
    Embrace the love that surrounds your soul,
In its warm embrace, you'll find yourself whole,
For you are needed, your presence, a light,
A beacon of hope, shining ever so bright.
    Know that you're not alone in this fight,
Others have battled and emerged into the light,

Together, we'll stand, united and strong,
With resilience and love, we'll conquer the wrong.

Hold onto hope, let it guide your way,
Through the darkest valleys, it will lead you to day,
You are worthy of a life filled with delight,
Of joy, laughter, and dreams taking flight.

The beauty of tomorrow lies in your hands,
In the love that surrounds you, across the lands,
You are a masterpiece, a precious creation,
Embrace life's blessings, and find liberation.

So, my dear, stay with us, don't let go,
For your journey is far from finished, you know,
Let love heal your wounds, and hope be your guide,
Together, we'll triumph, side by side.

NINE

DON'T LOSE SIGHT

In the darkest nights, when shadows loom,
When hope feels lost, like a withered bloom,
Hold on, dear soul, don't let go,
For love surrounds you, more than you know.

You are cherished, precious, beyond compare,
A beacon of light in a world of despair.
Your heart holds dreams, waiting to be unfurled,
A tapestry of possibilities, yet to be twirled.

Embrace the beauty that awaits your eyes,
The sun-kissed mornings, the starlit skies.
For in your smile, there lies such grace,
A gentle warmth that can light up any space.

Reach out your hand, let others draw near,
For support and love can dissolve every fear.
Lean on the shoulders of those who care,
They'll hold you close, help you repair.

Know that storms pass, clouds will part,
And healing can come from the depths of your heart.
Your journey is not over, it's just begun,
With resilience and love, you'll rise like the sun.

So stay strong, dear one, don't lose sight,
Of the miracles that await in the morning light.
You have a purpose, a story to be told,
Hold onto hope, let your heart unfold.

TEN

STRENGTH TO ACHIEVE

In the darkest hour, when shadows loom,
And despair engulfs you like a gloom,
Hold on, dear soul, don't lose your way,
For hope's sweet light will guide your stay.

In life's vast tapestry, you have a thread,
A purpose unique, yet to be spread,
Embrace the journey, let your heart ignite,
For in your presence, the world finds delight.

When storms assail and tear your heart apart,
Remember, love can heal even the deepest scar,
Reach out to those who lend a helping hand,
Together, we'll navigate this treacherous land.

You are cherished, my dear, beyond compare,
A beacon of light in a world unfair,

The sky, the stars, they whisper your name,
For your existence, this world is forever changed.

Seek solace in the embrace of a friend,
Let them guide you through the darkness, to mend,
For in their warmth, you'll find the strength anew,
To rise above the pain and start anew.

Hold onto faith, for it will never cease,
It's the elixir of hope that grants release,
With every sunrise, a chance to begin,
To rewrite your story and let joy seep in.

So, my dear soul, don't surrender, don't fade,
For life's symphony still has a serenade,
You are loved, you are needed, please believe,
In the power of hope, and the strength to achieve.

ELEVEN

GENTLEST OF SOUNDS

In the darkest of nights, when hope seems to fade,
When the weight of the world becomes hard to evade,
Take solace, dear soul, in the stars up above,
For they whisper of beauty, of strength, and of love.

Hold on, my friend, to the light deep within,
For it's there that your spirit can truly begin,
To rise above sorrow, to conquer the pain,
And find solace in knowing you're not alone in this terrain.

Embrace the beauty that this life can bestow,
In the laughter of loved ones, in the places you go,
For your presence is valued, your worth unsurpassed,
And the world would be lesser without you, so vast.

Seek out the sunrise, let it paint your skies,
With hues of resilience, with hope that never dies,
For in every new dawn, there's a chance to renew,

To find strength in your heart, and your dreams to pursue.

Hold on, my dear, to the love that surrounds,
In the warmth of a touch, in the gentlest of sounds,
For love is a beacon, a guide through the night,
A reminder that you are worthy, that you shine so bright.

Remember, my friend, that there's help to be found,
In the arms of a friend, in a voice, soft and sound,
Reach out, let them hold you, let their love be your shield,
For together we'll triumph, and darkness will yield.

Hold on, stay strong, let love guide your way,
For the beauty that awaits you will brighten each day,
You are cherished, dear soul, never forget,
In this journey called life, you're not alone, not just yet.

TWELVE

REACH OUT

In the depths of darkness, you may find,
A flicker of hope, a guiding light,
For within your heart, a strength resides,
A resilience that cannot be denied.

When shadows cast their heavy weight,
And life's burdens seem too great,
Remember, dear soul, you're not alone,
Reach out, seek help, let your pain be known.

For in sharing your story, you'll come to see,
The power of connection, the strength of unity,
Others have walked the path you tread,
They understand the thoughts that fill your head.

Hold onto hope, let it be your guide,
Embrace the love that's by your side,

You matter, dear one, in countless ways,
Your presence brings joy to others' days.

In the broken pieces, beauty can be found,
A chance for growth, a common ground,
Together, we can create a brighter tomorrow,
Where hope prevails over sorrow.

So when darkness looms, and despair draws near,
Remember, my friend, there's nothing to fear,
Reach out, hold on, let your voice be heard,
For in seeking help, your spirit will be stirred.

You are valued, cherished, and deeply loved,
A precious soul, blessed from above,
The world is better with you in it, you see,
Choose life, embrace hope, and set yourself free.

THIRTEEN

STRENGTH ANEW

In the depths of despair, when darkness surrounds,
And the weight on your heart feels too heavy to bear,
Remember, dear soul, you're not alone,
There's a world of love waiting, ready to care.

When the shadows consume you, obscuring the light,
And hope seems a distant and fading refrain,
Hold on, my friend, for the dawn will arrive,
With colors of healing, washing away the pain.

Embrace the strength that resides deep within,
A warrior's spirit, resilient and true,
Let the scars you carry be badges of honor,
Proof that you've faced battles and made it through.

Reach out your hand, let others guide you,
For in unity's embrace, we find strength anew,

Lean on the shoulders of those who love you,
Their support will carry you, help you pull through.
    Remember, dear heart, that life's worth living,
Despite the darkness, there's beauty to see,
The stars still shimmer, the flowers still bloom,
And your presence on earth is a precious decree.
    You are cherished, valued, and deeply adored,
A symphony of light in a world full of strife,
So hold on, stay strong, and believe in tomorrow,
For your story is unfinished, and it's filled with life.

FOURTEEN

YOU'RE NOT ALONE

In darkness deep, where shadows weave,
A soul in pain, afraid to grieve,
I offer you these words, my friend,
To guide you back, from your tragic end.

When hope seems lost, and skies turn gray,
Remember love will light the way.
In times of darkness, don't despair,
For love and hope are always there.

Reach out your hand, don't be alone,
Together we can find a home.
In every heart, a spark ignites,
A flame that burns through darkest nights.

Embrace the love that's all around,
Let it lift you from the ground.
For you are cherished, you are dear,
Your presence brings us joy and cheer.

Your story's not yet fully told,
A tale of courage, brave and bold.
Hold on, stay strong, and believe,
Tomorrow's gifts you'll soon receive.

Life's journey is a winding road,
With beauty yet to be bestowed.
So take my hand and walk with me,
For brighter days are yet to see.

In life's embrace, find solace deep,
And may your heart, in love, find keep.
Remember, friend, you're not alone,
Together, we will find our own.

FIFTEEN

TRUST IN TOMORROW

In the darkest hours, when shadows loom,
And pain engulfs your weary soul,
Know that you're not alone in this fight,
For love and support will make you whole.

In the depths of despair, when hope seems lost,
Remember, dear one, your worth is vast.
Your presence brings joy, your smile a light,
You are cherished, valued, and loved, steadfast.

Hold on, my friend, and stay strong,
For tomorrow holds a brand new song.
Your story is not yet fully told,
Brighter days await, watch them unfold.

Reach out your hand, let others in,
Together we'll conquer the storm within.

In unity, we find strength and grace,
Together we'll rise, embracing life's embrace.
    Believe in the power that lies within,
To heal, to grow, to rise again.
You are a warrior, brave and true,
And the world is better because of you.
    So hold on tight, don't let go,
There is help and support, you need to know.
You are not alone, we'll walk this path,
With love and hope, we'll conquer the wrath.
    Stay with us, dear soul, let your light shine,
For you are cherished, a gift divine.
Embrace the love that surrounds you now,
And let it guide you, through darkness, somehow.
    Remember, my friend, you're never alone,
Together we'll find a way to atone.
Hold on, stay strong, and trust in tomorrow,
For your presence in this world, we'll forever borrow.

SIXTEEN

SO MUCH MORE

In the darkest night, when shadows loom,
And thoughts of despair start to consume,
Remember, my friend, you're not alone,
There's love and support waiting to be shown.

    Hold on tight, and don't let go,
For within your heart, a flame does glow,
A light that shines for all to see,
A beacon of hope, forever free.

    Though the road is tough, and tears may fall,
Know that you're cherished, one and all,
Your presence is a gift, a precious treasure,
A soul that brings joy beyond measure.

    Reach out your hand, let others in,
Together we'll conquer the battles within,

For in unity lies strength and might,
And love will guide us through the darkest night.

The world may seem cruel, unfair, and unkind,
But beauty and wonder, you're bound to find,
In the laughter of children, the colors of dawn,
In the embrace of loved ones, you'll carry on.

Believe in tomorrow, for it holds the key,
To the dreams and hopes you're destined to see,
Your story is not over, it's just begun,
Embrace the journey, for you're not yet done.

So, my dear friend, please hold on tight,
You're worthy of love, you're a shining light,
Don't let the darkness cloud your view,
For there's so much more, waiting for you.

SEVENTEEN

TOGETHER WE ARE STRONG

In the shadows of despair, I see your weary soul,
Lost in a storm of sorrow, longing to be whole.
But hold on, my dear friend, for life still has much to give,
In the depths of your darkness, a flickering light shall live.

When the weight becomes too heavy, and hope starts to fade,
Remember, there are hands reaching out, eager to aid.
In the embrace of love, find solace and respite,
Let the warmth of compassion guide you through the night.

You are not alone, though the clouds may block the sun,
Together, we'll weather this storm, until it's finally

done.
For your existence holds a beauty, unique and true,
A tapestry of dreams and passions, waiting to shine through.

The world yearns for your laughter, your smile so bright,
A beacon of strength, illuminating the darkest night.
Reach out, my dear friend, don't let the darkness win,
For in unity and love, we'll find the strength within.

So, hold on to the fragile thread of hope, my friend,
Let love and support heal what seems to have no end.
Though the road may be treacherous, and the journey long,
Know that you are cherished, and together we are strong.

EIGHTEEN

BEACON OF HOPE

In the depths of despair, when shadows grow long,
Hold on to the strength and let hope sing its song.
For you are not alone, though darkness may surround,
There are hearts that care, waiting to be found.

In the quiet moments, when the night feels so cold,
Remember, dear friend, you have a hand to hold.
Through the storms of life, when it's hard to see,
There is love that waits, patient as can be.

Your presence, a light, shines brighter than you know,
A tapestry of beauty, with seeds yet to sow.
The world needs your laughter, your heart's gentle embrace,
Your dreams and your passions, your unique grace.

Though the road may be tough, and the journey

unclear,
Know that there's strength in you, to overcome fear.
Reach out, dear soul, to those who understand,
For together we'll rise, hand in hand.

Believe in tomorrow, for it holds so much more,
The promise of healing, and joy to explore.
Hold tight to the love that surrounds you each day,
For you are cherished, in every possible way.

You have the power to rise above the pain,
To find solace and hope, even in the rain.
So let this be a reminder, a lifeline of love,
That you matter, dear friend, in this world you're part of.

Hold on, stay strong, for your story's not done,
Embrace the sunrise, for a new day has begun.
You are worthy, you are loved, and you're meant to be,
A beacon of hope, shining eternally.

NINETEEN

WE'LL RISE AND LEARN TO COPE

In the darkest hour, when shadows grow,
When pain engulfs and tears freely flow,
Hold on, dear soul, don't let go just yet,
For there's a world of love you haven't met.

Though storms may rage and clouds hang low,
Within your heart, a light does glow.
You're not alone in this battle, my friend,
Together, we'll find strength to mend.

Life's beauty lies in the simplest things,
The gentle touch of a loved one's wings,
The laughter shared, the friendships true,
In every sunrise, a promise to renew.

Hold on, stay strong, believe in tomorrow,
For in the darkest night, hope will follow.

You're precious, unique, a treasure untold,
Your presence in this world, worth more than gold.
    Through valleys deep and mountains high,
We'll journey together, you and I.
With love as our guide, we'll conquer the strife,
And find healing and joy in this precious life.
    So take my hand, let's rise above,
Embrace the journey, embrace the love.
Hold on to that fragile thread of hope,
For together, we'll rise and learn to cope.

TWENTY

LET YOUR STORY UNFOLD

In the darkest hours, when shadows loom,
And despair engulfs your weary soul,
Remember, my friend, you're not alone,
For love surrounds you, making you whole.

Though the road may be rugged and steep,
And tears may stain your weary face,
Believe in tomorrow, have faith in your strength,
Hold on tight, embrace life's embrace.

The world may seem cold and unforgiving,
But within it lies beauty, waiting to be seen,
In the laughter of children, the warmth of a smile,
In the gentle touch that mends and redeems.

You are unique, a masterpiece divine,
With a heart that beats to its own sweet song,

Your presence in this world, it matters so much,
You're cherished, valued, and forever belong.

Reach out your hand, let others lend theirs,
Together we'll conquer the darkness within,
Find solace in simplest joys, embrace the journey,
And let the healing of love and connection begin.

Hold on to hope, rise above the pain,
For tomorrow holds the promise of a brand new day,
With every breath, let your spirit soar high,
And find the strength to chase your dreams away.

You're worthy, dear friend, of love and of light,
Let the darkness fade, let your spirit ignite,
For life is a gift, a precious treasure to hold,
Embrace it, cherish it, let your story unfold.

TWENTY-ONE

HOLD ON

In the darkest hour, when shadows loom,
Remember, dear soul, you're not alone in this room.
Though pain may grip your heart, like a vise tight,
There's still a glimmer of hope, a flickering light.

    Hold on, my friend, for the world needs your grace,
Your presence, your spirit, your unique embrace.
In this tapestry of life, you have a vital role,
To touch hearts, inspire, and make others whole.

    Love is a balm that can heal the deepest scars,
Embrace its warmth, let it mend your shattered parts.
Reach out to those around, let them be your guide,
Together, we'll conquer the darkness deep inside.

    The journey may seem long, the path unclear,
But know that tomorrow holds promise, my dear.

Each sunrise brings new beginnings, a chance to grow,
To find solace in simple joys, and let your spirit glow.
You are cherished, valued, a soul of worth,
Your story's not finished, there's more to unearth.
So stay strong, hold on, and believe in your might,
For your presence in this world, it shines so bright.
Let the beauty of life dance before your eyes,
Embrace the love that surrounds you, let it rise.
Cherish each moment, let your spirit soar,
For you are deserving, and you belong evermore.

TWENTY-TWO

CHERISHED PEARL

In the darkest hour, when shadows loom,
And hope seems lost in the gathering gloom,
Remember, dear soul, you're not alone,
For love's embrace is waiting to be shown.

    Your existence holds a beauty yet untold,
A story of resilience, waiting to unfold.
Though pain may grip your fragile heart,
Believe in tomorrow, for healing will start.

    Hold on, my dear, stay strong and true,
The world needs your light, it needs you.
With every sunrise, a new beginning awaits,
And the promise of joy, as sorrow abates.

    In unity and compassion, find your strength,
Reach out to others, let love's power extend.

For in connection, we find solace and grace,
A tapestry of support, a sacred space.
    Embrace the journey, let your spirit shine,
You are cherished, valued, and forever divine.
Your worth knows no bounds, it's a truth profound,
You are worthy of love, on this earth you are crowned.
    Your story is not finished, there's more to be told,
In this vast world, you have a place to behold.
So hold onto hope, let your heart unfurl,
For you are a precious gem, a cherished pearl.

TWENTY-THREE

REASON TO PERSEVERE

In the darkest depths, where shadows reside,
A flicker of hope, let it be your guide.
For you are not alone, dear broken soul,
In this vast universe, hearts are intertwined, whole.

Hold on, my friend, stay strong and true,
Believe in tomorrow, for it holds something new.
Each sunrise brings promise, a chance to heal,
To find joy in the moments, let your spirit reveal.

Embrace the journey, let your light shine bright,
For your presence in this world, it brings delight.
You are unique, a gem with stories untold,
A tapestry of memories, waiting to unfold.

In unity we stand, compassion in our hearts,
Together we can conquer the darkest of arts.

Reach out, dear soul, let others lend a hand,
For love and support, they're always close at hand.

Cherish each moment, for life's beauty lies,
In the laughter, the tears, and the endless skies.
Your story's not finished, there's still much to see,
You have a place in this world, a purpose to be.

So hold onto hope, let your heart unfurl,
You're a precious gem, a cherished pearl.
You matter, dear soul, more than you know,
In this symphony of life, your presence has a glow.

Remember, my friend, when darkness is near,
There's always a reason to persevere.
Let love be your anchor, your guiding star,
For in this vast universe, you are never too far.

TWENTY-FOUR

BATTLE IS WON

In the darkest hours, when shadows loom,
And despair whispers a haunting tune,
Hold on, dear soul, stay strong, I plea,
For there's a world of hope that surrounds thee.

Embrace the journey, let your spirit soar,
Find solace in the simple joys life has in store.
For every sunrise paints a brand new day,
Where dreams can flourish and fears can sway.

Know that you are cherished, valued, and adored,
A precious gem in this symphony, never ignored.
Your presence, like a ripple, creates waves of light,
Bringing warmth and love, banishing the night.

Unleash the power of unity and compassion's embrace,
Let others lift you up, seeking solace and grace.

For in the tapestry of life, we're woven as one,
Supporting each other until the battle is won.

Your story is not finished, there's more to be found,
In every smile, in every heartbeat's sound.
Hold onto hope, let your heart unfurl,
For you are a warrior, a beacon in this world.

Believe in tomorrow, for it holds a promise true,
A symphony of possibilities, crafted just for you.
You're deserving of love, of laughter, and of light,
So stay, dear soul, and let your spirit take flight.

TWENTY-FIVE

MENDING YOUR HEART

In the depths of despair, where shadows reside,
There lies a flicker, a flame deep inside.
Though darkness surrounds you, I beg you to see,
A world full of beauty, a life yet to be.

Hold on to that flicker, let it guide your way,
For even the smallest light can brighten the gray.
You're not alone in this fight, my dear friend,
There are hands reaching out, ready to mend.

In a world that seems cruel, where hope seems lost,
Remember your worth, no matter the cost.
You're unique, you're precious, a masterpiece true,
And this world would be darker without the beauty of you.

Embrace the journey, the ups and the downs,

For strength lies within you, where courage abounds.
Find solace in laughter, in music, in art,
Let love guide your steps, mending your heart.

    You're cherished, you're valued, don't ever forget,
The impact you've made, the lives you have met.
Your story's not over, there's more left to tell,
Unleash your potential, and break free from this spell.

    Together we stand, united as one,
With love, compassion, the battle is won.
Believe in tomorrow, for it holds the key,
To a future of hope, where you're meant to be.

TWENTY-SIX

YOU DESERVE TO STAY

In the depths of despair, where shadows reside,
A flicker of hope, let it be your guide.
For your heart holds a story, yet to unfold,
A tale of resilience, waiting to be told.

In this vast universe, you're a star so bright,
With a unique purpose, you bring forth light.
Your presence is cherished, your worth immense,
Embrace the journey, let love be your defense.

Find solace in simple joys, the sun's warm embrace,
The laughter of loved ones, a gentle embrace.
Hold onto hope, like a lifeline in the storm,
For you're not alone, together we'll transform.

In unity, compassion, we shall rise above,
Supporting each other with unwavering love.

Your pain may be heavy, but you're strong inside,
Believe in your power, don't let hope subside.
   Cherish each moment, for life's a precious gift,
Let your spirit shine, let your soul uplift.
Your story's not finished, there's still much to be,
Break free from despair, embrace your destiny.
   You're a masterpiece, a work of art divine,
The beauty you bring, no boundaries can define.
So, hold on, dear soul, let the darkness fade away,
For you are valued, and you deserve to stay.

TWENTY-SEVEN

LETTING HEALING BEGIN

In the darkest of nights, when shadows loom,
And despair engulfs you, like gathering gloom,
Hold onto hope, let it light your way,
For there's a brighter dawn, a brand-new day.

Your journey, my friend, is not yet complete,
In this vast universe, your purpose, so sweet,
Embrace the unknown, with courage and might,
Unleash your spirit, let it take flight.

You are not alone, in this battle you face,
Together we stand, with love and embrace,
United we'll conquer the darkness within,
Transforming our pain, letting healing begin.

Your worth is immeasurable, your potential untold,
The impact you've made, more precious than gold,

Believe in tomorrow, in promise it holds,
Let your spirit shine, as your story unfolds.
    Hold onto the love, the compassion, the care,
For in these connections, strength we will share,
Your resilience, your strength, they're a guiding light,
Embrace your destiny, let your soul take flight.
    So, my dear friend, in this moment so tough,
Hold on to the hope, for life is enough,
You are valued, you're cherished, you're needed here,
Embrace the beauty you bring, banish the fear.
    In unity we'll triumph, in love we'll prevail,
Let your spirit soar, as you set sail,
Know that you matter, you're never alone,
Together, we'll conquer, and find our way home.

TWENTY-EIGHT

MORE THAN WORDS

In the darkest hours, when shadows loom,
And despair engulfs you like a tomb,
Know that you're not alone in this fight,
Together, we'll chase away the night.

Embrace your journey, hold onto hope,
In this vast universe, you're not a mere trope.
Your story's not finished, there's much to be seen,
A tapestry of life, woven bold and serene.

You are a flame, a spark divine,
Unleash your potential, let your spirit shine.
Break free from the chains that bind your soul,
Embrace the light, let your dreams unfold.

In unity we find strength, compassion our guide,
Love's healing touch, a balm for wounds inside.
Reach out to those who lend a helping hand,
Together, we'll rise, like phoenixes we'll stand.

Believe in tomorrow, it holds a promise bright,
A world of wonders, where you'll take flight.
Your worth is immeasurable, your value so grand,
In this tapestry of life, you have a place, unplanned.

The storm may rage, but you're stronger than before,
Resilience within you, an unyielding core.
Let your spirit soar, embrace your destiny,
You're cherished, you're needed, you're wanted, you see.

Hold on, dear friend, for life's beauty awaits,
In the whispers of love, in the hands of fate.
You are valued, you matter, more than words can express,
Stay with us, dear soul, and let your light impress.

TWENTY-NINE

IMMEASURABLE

In the depths of despair, where shadows dwell,
A flicker of hope, I wish to tell.
When darkness surrounds and tears fill your eyes,
Remember, dear soul, you're a star in the skies.

In this vast universe, you have a place,
A story to share, a light to embrace.
Though storms may rage and winds may blow,
Your strength will guide you, this I know.

Hold onto hope, let it be your guide,
For brighter days are waiting outside.
Reach out to others, let love be your shield,
Together we'll conquer, refusing to yield.

You are not alone in this daunting fight,
A community standing by, day and night.
We'll hold your hand through the darkest night,
And lead you towards the morning light.

Your worth is immeasurable, your heart so pure,
You're a masterpiece, of that I'm sure.
Your smile, your laughter, they bring joy to all,
In this vast tapestry, you stand tall.

So, dear friend, embrace your journey ahead,
With love, with hope, let your spirit be fed.
Believe in tomorrow's promise, let your light shine,
For your story's not over, it's just begun to intertwine.

THIRTY

OVERCOME THE PAIN

In the depths of despair, when darkness surrounds,
Hold on, my dear friend, for hope still abounds.
In this vast universe, you're not alone,
A tapestry of hearts, together we've grown.

    Each life is a melody, unique and rare,
A symphony of stories, we all have a share.
Though pain may consume, and tears may fall,
There's strength in our unity, a beacon for all.

    Let compassion be your guide, a balm for the soul,
Reach out to others, let empathy unfold.
For in lifting each other, we find our own worth,
A testament to resilience, our collective rebirth.

    Remember, dear one, you're cherished and adored,
Your presence on this Earth, a gift to be explored.

Your journey's not over, there's more yet to see,
The beauty of tomorrow, waiting to be free.

So embrace the sunrise, let it warm your face,
Embrace the love around you, in every embrace.
For you are valued, you matter, in countless ways,
Together, we'll conquer the darkest of days.

Hold on, my dear friend, let your light shine bright,
For in your existence, the world finds its light.
We stand beside you, through the storm we'll remain,
United in compassion, we'll overcome the pain.

THIRTY-ONE

BRAND-NEW DAY

In the depths of despair, when shadows grow long,
Hold on, dear soul, for this is not your song.
Embrace the journey, let your spirit rise,
For in your heart, a flame of hope never dies.

You are not alone, though darkness may surround,
A community stands by, love tightly wound.
Together we'll weather the storm's mighty roar,
With hands interlocked, we'll reach the distant shore.

In the tapestry of life, your thread weaves a tale,
A masterpiece of strength, resilience, and travail.
Your presence is a gift, a light to behold,
A testament to the worth of a soul untold.

Find solace in love, let its warmth embrace,
In art's gentle embrace, find solace and grace.

Believe in your potential, for greatness lies within,
Unleash your dreams, let your journey begin.

Remember, dear heart, your worth can't be measured,
Your beauty, immeasurable, a treasure forever.
Though shadows may linger, the sun will rise anew,
Embrace the promise of tomorrow, it's waiting for you.

Hold on, my friend, let your light shine bright,
For even in the darkest of days, there is a glimmer of light.
Together, with love and compassion, we'll find a way,
To overcome the darkest nights, and welcome a brand-new day.

THIRTY-TWO

BRIGHTER TOMORROW

In the depths of darkness, when hope seems lost,
And shadows consume each moment, a heavy cost.
Hold on, dear soul, for you are not alone,
In this journey of life, together we have grown.

Embrace your worth, your spirit so bright,
A beacon of light, even in the darkest night.
Believe in your potential, your dreams untold,
For within your heart, a fire does unfold.

Love surrounds you, like a warm embrace,
Community support, a shelter in this race.
Reach out, dear one, let others lend a hand,
Together we'll rise, against the tide we'll stand.

In the solace of art, find refuge and peace,
Express your pain, let your worries release.

Your journey, unique, with lessons to learn,
Unleash your passions, let your dreams return.
    For you are a gift, a treasure untold,
Your presence on Earth, a story to unfold.
The world needs your light, your love, and your grace,
A tapestry of souls, each playing their own space.
    Tomorrow holds promise, a new day will dawn,
With resilience and strength, we'll carry on.
You are valued, you are cherished, it's true,
Hold on, dear one, for a brighter tomorrow awaits you.

THIRTY-THREE

UNIQUE MASTERPIECE

In the depths of despair, when darkness surrounds,
Hold on, my friend, for hope still abounds.
In your heart, a flame flickers bright,
A beacon of strength, a guiding light.

You're not alone in this weary fight,
A community stands, embracing the night.
Reach out, dear soul, let others in,
Together we'll rise, stronger than sin.

Know your worth, like a diamond, you shine,
A unique masterpiece, one of a kind.
The world needs your smile, your laughter, your voice,
A symphony of hope, a melody of choice.

Embrace your journey, the highs and the lows,
For in every stumble, resilience grows.

Through valleys of sorrow, you'll find your way,
To mountains of joy, where your spirit will sway.
    Let love be your armor, your shield from despair,
A reminder that others genuinely care.
And when the storm rages, and tears start to fall,
Know that tomorrow holds promise for all.
    Your presence on Earth is a gift to be cherished,
A canvas for dreams, yet to be nourished.
So hold on, dear friend, let your light shine,
For a new day awaits, with blessings divine.
    Remember, you're stronger than you'll ever know,
And the world is here, ready to help you grow.
You're not alone, this battle we'll win,
Believe in yourself, let your journey begin.

THIRTY-FOUR

RESILIENCE RESIDES

In the darkest night, when shadows loom,
Hold on, dear soul, for brighter days will bloom.
Though pain may grip your heart with heavy weight,
Know that love surrounds you, it's never too late.

Embrace your journey, let hope be your guide,
For within your spirit, resilience resides.
Each step you take, a testament of your might,
You're not alone, we'll walk with you, day and night.

In the depths of sorrow, art can heal,
Let creativity flow, let it be your shield.
Paint your emotions, sing your heart's song,
Express the depths within you, where you belong.

Your life, a masterpiece, unique and rare,
A tapestry woven with love and care.

Though clouds may obscure the sun's golden light,
Believe in tomorrow, it holds promise, so bright.

Reach out to others, let compassion mend,
For in unity, we find strength to transcend.
Together we'll build a world where hearts can mend,
Where every soul finds solace, a true friend.

Hold on, dear one, for this world needs your light,
Your story, your laughter, your courage, shining bright.
In the symphony of life, your voice is profound,
You matter, dear soul, your presence is profound.

So, stay with us, embrace the love that's near,
For your journey is valuable, don't disappear.
Hold on, dear soul, let hope be your guide,
A brighter future awaits, just on the other side.

THIRTY-FIVE

TAPESTRY OF LIFE

In the darkest hour, when shadows fall,
And despair engulfs your weary soul,
Remember, dear one, you're not alone,
For love and hope are always known.

    Life's burdens may seem too much to bear,
But hold on tight, release your despair.
For in this world, there lies a place,
Where hearts can mend, and souls find solace.

    Though pain may bind you, like chains so tight,
Believe in tomorrow, embrace the light.
The world needs your laughter, your gentle touch,
Your presence, dear one, it means so much.

    Reach out your hand, let others see,
The strength within you, waiting to be free.

For in the embrace of a caring soul,
New beginnings emerge, making you whole.
    The road may be long, the journey hard,
But remember, dear one, you hold the card.
Your life is a canvas, waiting to bloom,
With colors of hope, dispelling the gloom.
    So when the darkness threatens to consume,
Seek out the light, let it break through.
For in this vast tapestry of life,
Your story matters, it's worth the fight.
    Hold on, dear one, let your heart unfold,
There's love in this world, waiting to be told.
Together we stand, united we'll be,
For you are not alone, you are loved, you see.

ABOUT THE AUTHOR

Walter the Educator is one of the pseudonyms for Walter Anderson. Formally educated in Chemistry, Business, and Education, he is an educator, an author, a diverse entrepreneur, and he is the son of a disabled war veteran. "Walter the Educator" shares his time between educating and creating. He holds interests and owns several creative projects that entertain, enlighten, enhance, and educate, hoping to inspire and motivate you.

Follow, find new works, and stay up to date
with Walter the Educator™
at WaltertheEducator.com

www.ingramcontent.com/pod-product-compliance
Lightning Source LLC
LaVergne TN
LVHW051958060526
838201LV00059B/3724